PLAGUE!

Lynn Peppas

Crabtree Publishing Company
www.crabtreebooks.com

Crabtree Publishing Company

www.crabtreebooks.com

Author: Lynn Peppas
Publishing plan research and development: Sean Charlebois, Reagan Miller Crabtree Publishing Company
Photo research: Robin Johnson
Editors: Sonya Newland, Kathy Middleton
Proofreader: Crystal Sikkens
Design: Tim Mayer (Mayer Media)
Cover design: Ken Wright
Production coordinator and prepress technician: Ken Wright
Print coordinator: Katherine Berti

Produced for Crabtree Publishing by White-Thomson Publishing

Picture Credits:
Alamy: Interfoto: p. 14; The Art Archive: p. 15; North Wind Picture Archive: pp. 22–23; SOTK2011: p. 37; Imagebroker: pp. 42–43; **Corbis**: pp. 4–5; Alfredo Dagli Orti/The Art Archive: pp. 3, 18–19; Lebrecht Authors/Lebrecht Music & Arts: pp. 10–11; Bettmann: pp. 20–21, 41; Heritage Images: pp. 26–27; Kapoor Baldev/Sygma: p. 43; **Dreamstime**: Johnnydevil: pp. 44–45; **Getty Images**: pp. 7, 8–9, 10, 16–17, 38–39; The Bridgeman Art Library: pp. 30–31, 34–35; Peter Willi: p. 40; **Shutterstock**: back cover; anatolypareev: p. 6; Sergejus Byckovskis: p. 8; **Topfoto**: The Granger Collection: pp. 12–13; Ann Ronan Picture Library/HIP: p. 25; **Wikipedia**: pp. 1, 28, 29, 32, 36; Rita Greer: front cover; Liber Chronicarum/Die Schedelsche Weltchronik: p. 24; Walters Art Museum: p. 33.

Library and Archives Canada Cataloguing in Publication

Peppas, Lynn
Plague! / Lynn Peppas.

(Crabtree chrome)
Includes index.
Issued also in electronic formats.
ISBN 978-0-7787-1102-5 (bound).--ISBN 978-0-7787-1122-3 (pbk.)

1. Plague--History--Juvenile literature. 2. Black Death--Juvenile
literature. 3. Medicine, Medieval--Juvenile literature.
I. Title. II. Series: Crabtree chrome

RC172 P47 2013 j614.5'732 C2013-900271-5

Library of Congress Cataloging-in-Publication Data

CIP available at Library of Congress

Crabtree Publishing Company

Printed in Canada/022013/BF20130114

www.crabtreebooks.com 1-800-387-7650

Published in Canada
Crabtree Publishing
616 Welland Ave.
St. Catharines, ON
L2M 5V6

Published in the United States
Crabtree Publishing
PMB 59051
350 Fifth Avenue, 59th Floor
New York, New York 10118

Published in the United Kingdom
Crabtree Publishing
Maritime House
Basin Road North, Hove
BN41 1WR

Published in Australia
Crabtree Publishing
3 Charles Street
Coburg North
VIC 3058

Contents

The Black Death

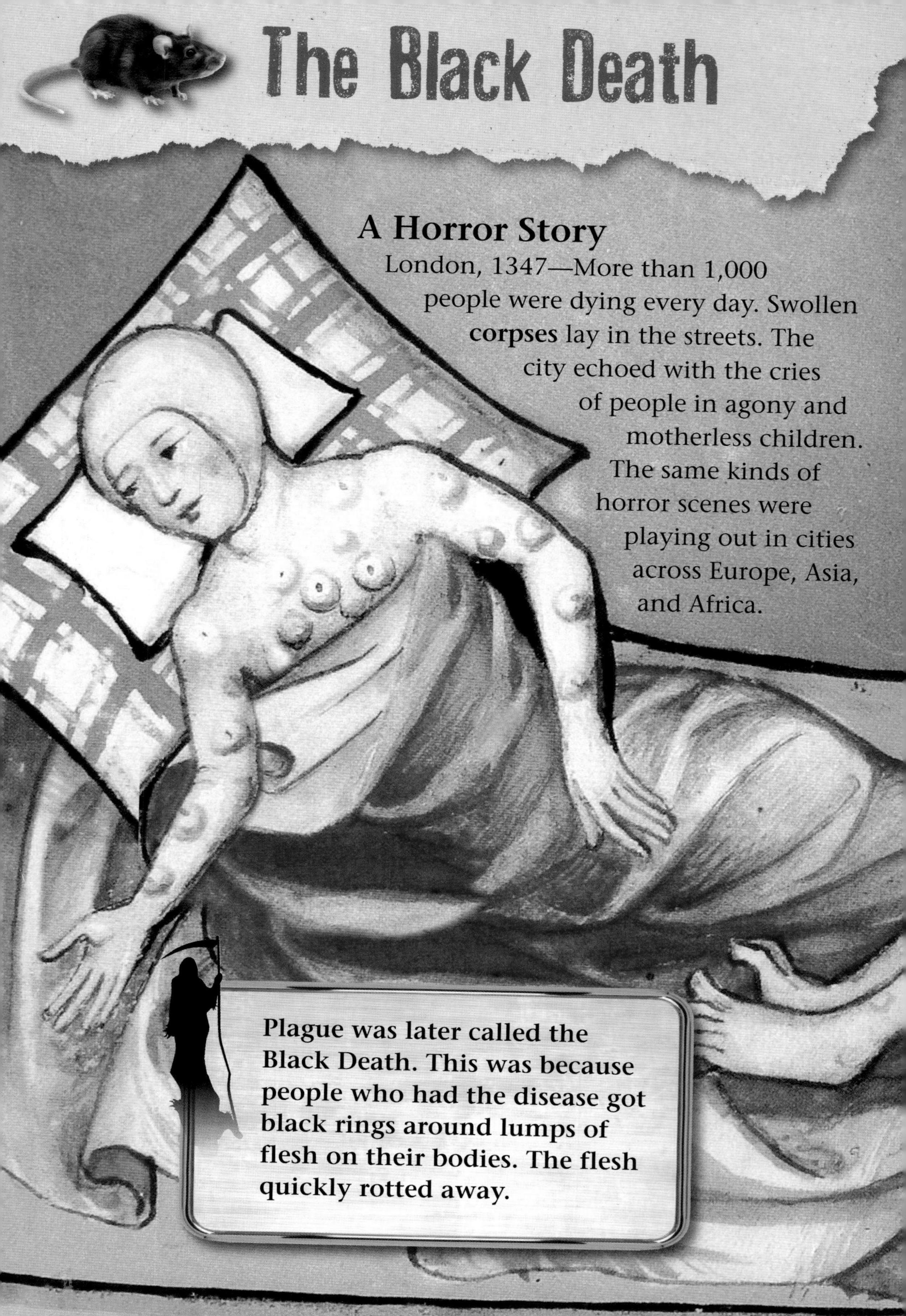

A Horror Story

London, 1347—More than 1,000 people were dying every day. Swollen **corpses** lay in the streets. The city echoed with the cries of people in agony and motherless children. The same kinds of horror scenes were playing out in cities across Europe, Asia, and Africa.

Plague was later called the Black Death. This was because people who had the disease got black rings around lumps of flesh on their bodies. The flesh quickly rotted away.

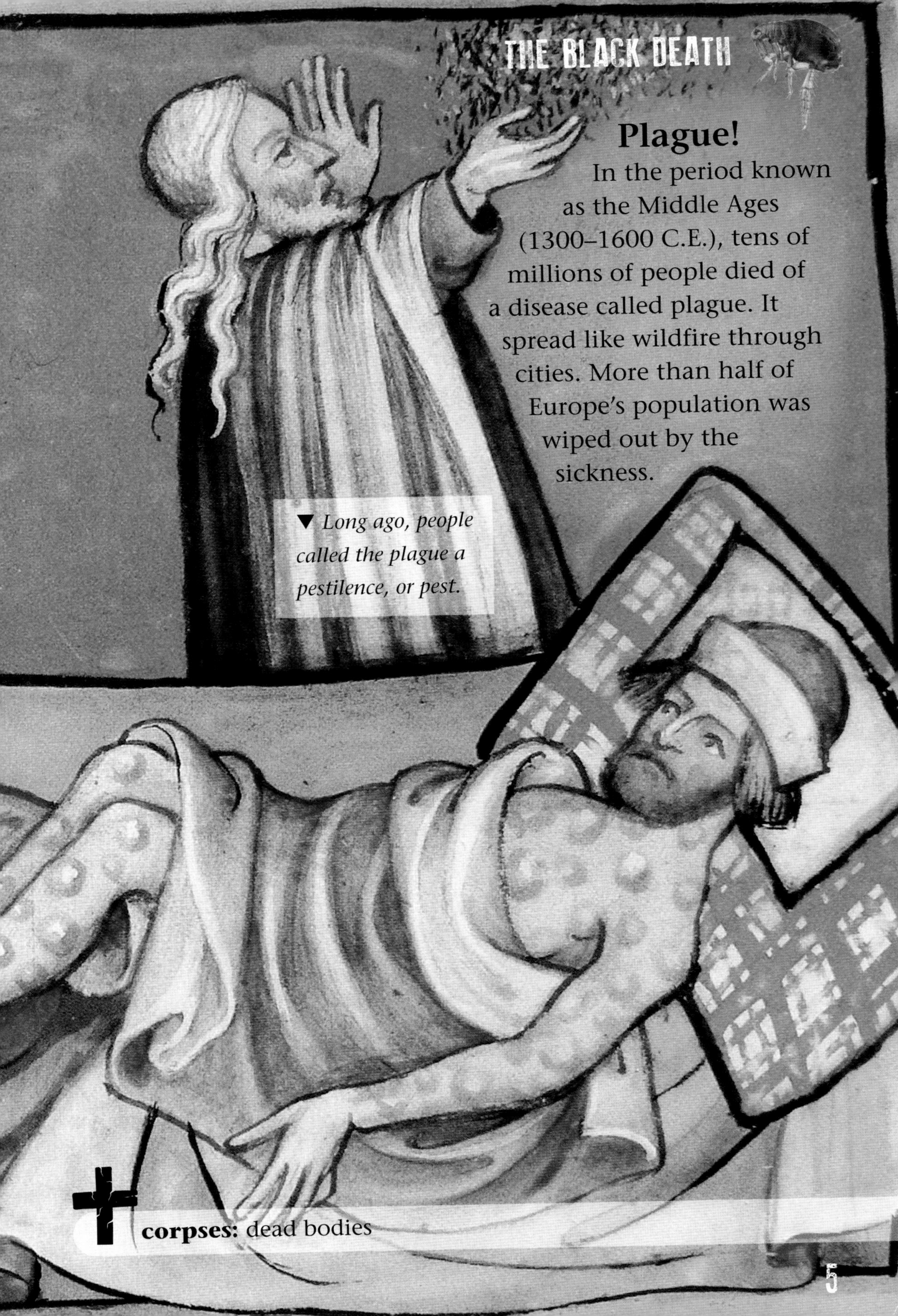

Plague!

In the period known as the Middle Ages (1300–1600 C.E.), tens of millions of people died of a disease called plague. It spread like wildfire through cities. More than half of Europe's population was wiped out by the sickness.

▼ *Long ago, people called the plague a pestilence, or pest.*

corpses: dead bodies

You Dirty Rat!

No one knew it at the time, but **rodents**, such as rats, carried plague. Some rats were immune to it. This meant that they could carry and pass on the disease without getting sick and dying from it themselves. Sometimes, natural events such as floods made plague-carrying rodents move into new areas.

▲ *Rats can live almost anywhere. In cities today, millions of them live in underground tunnels and other dark places.*

Spreading Plague

Plague spread in the cities when diseased rats passed the disease onto rats that were not immune. Those rats became sick and died. In the Middle Ages, rats were everywhere. People were used to living with them.

◀ *In the Middle Ages, rats thrived in the dirty city streets. No one realized they were the ones spreading the deadly disease.*

Alexandre Yersin was a Swiss-French scientist. In 1894, he discovered that rats carried plague. Before then, nobody knew how the disease was spread.

rodents: animals with fanglike teeth that are used for chewing

From Rats to Humans

Humans don't catch plague directly from the rodent. They catch it from the fleas that live on the **infected** rat. Fleas are small insects that live on warm-blooded animals such as rats and humans. Fleas bite animals and drink their blood for food. The blood is where the disease is carried.

◀ *There are more than 1,000 different kinds of fleas. About 100 of them can carry plague, including the human flea and the Oriental rat flea.*

Making the Jump

When the infected rodents died, the fleas that lived on them jumped to another animal to find fresh blood. Sometimes they jumped onto humans. The fleas bit the people and passed the disease on to them. To people living in the Middle Ages, fleas were as common as rats.

Fleas can jump about six inches (15 cm) from side to side, and about four inches (10 cm) upward. They leap from one living creature to another.

▼*This picture is called "The Dance of Death." Death is shown as skeletons dancing and playing instruments.*

infected: having a disease

No Care, No Cure

During the Middle Ages, doctors had no idea how to treat diseases such as plague. Many of them were afraid of catching it themselves. They ran away and left their patients behind. Everyone was terrified. People who did catch plague suffered and died in agony.

◄ *Throughout the Middle Ages, plague broke out in cities across Europe. This picture shows plague victims in Paris, the capital of France, in 1544.*

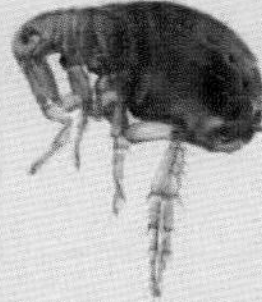

Deadliest Plague

There are three main kinds of plague. Each one has different **symptoms**. Septicemic plague is the rarest, but deadliest. People can catch septicemic plague from bites by infected fleas. In the Middle Ages, this type of plague was a death sentence. No one survived the killer disease.

Septicemic plague was not only the deadliest, it also killed people the quickest. Victims of septicemic plague died less than a day after catching it.

▼ *Many doctors, priests, and rich people packed up and left when the Black Death came to their cities.*

symptoms: the signs that someone has a particular illness

Pneumonic Plague

Pneumonic plague is a disease that begins in the chest. The victim's lungs fill with fluid making them feel as if they are drowning. Symptoms include chest pains, a terrible headache, and a high fever. Victims knew they were close to death when they started coughing up blood.

Catching Plague

Pneumonic plague is the most **contagious** type. People can catch it by breathing in the germs from a cough or sneeze of someone infected with the disease. People suffering from pneumonic plague would not have lived more than a day or two in the Middle Ages.

◀ *No one survived pneumonic plague. This painting from the Middle Ages shows people burying plague victims.*

"I ... buried my five children with my own hands ... So many died that all believed it was the end of the world."

Agnolo di Tura, an Italian writer

contagious: a disease that is spread by being near an infected person

Bubonic Plague

Bubonic plague is the most common type. It is the mildest form, but it is still a terrible disease. People catch bubonic plague from flea bites. Symptoms included a headache, high fever, chills, and extreme tiredness. Large lumps called buboes grow in the neck, armpit, or **groin** area of victims.

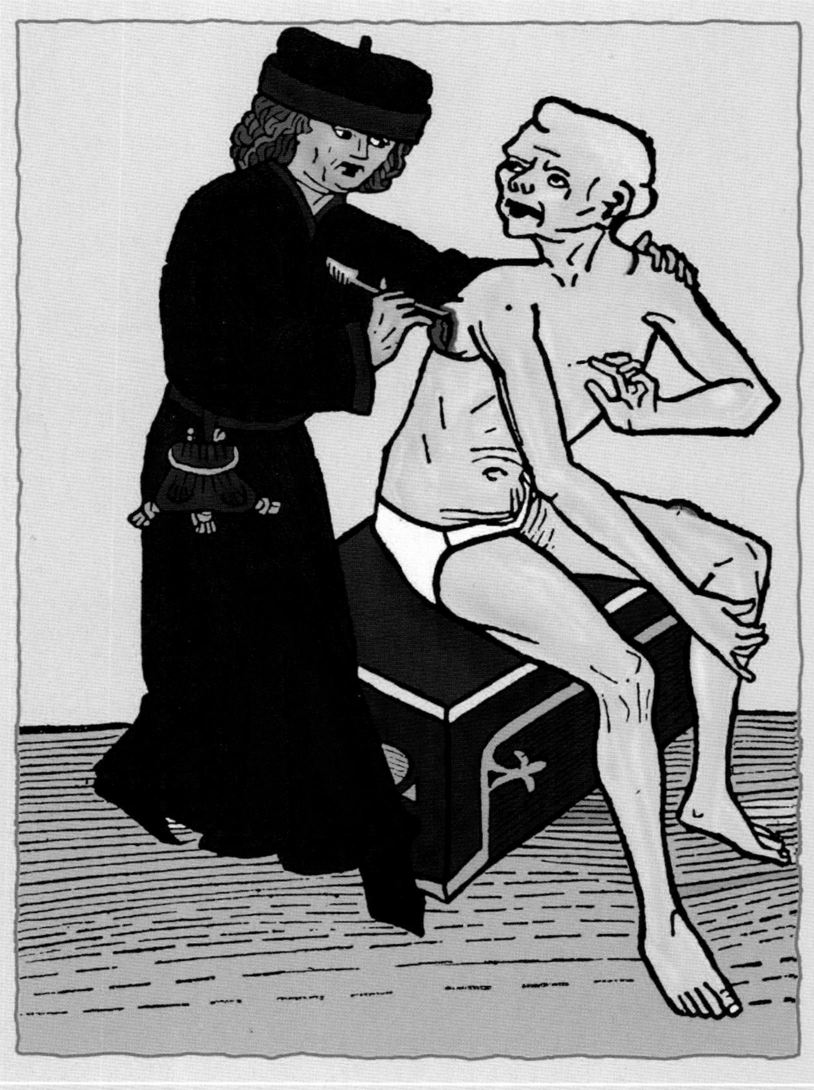

▲ *Doctors would cut open a patient's buboes to try to release the poison.*

Pus-filled Buboes

Buboes could grow up to four inches (10 cm)—about the size of a small apple. They were filled with a sticky, yellowish-white pus. Buboes were very painful when touched. Sometimes the muscle and flesh around the buboes would rot and turn black.

◀ *Buboes looked like large blisters or boils. They smelled terrible when they were cut open.*

In the Middle Ages, people had less than a 40 percent chance of surviving bubonic plague. But these were still better odds than surviving septicemic or pneumonic plague.

groin: the part of the body between the stomach and thigh

Spreading Death

Natural Boundaries

Mountains, oceans, and rivers act as natural **boundaries** between cities and countries. Long ago, people did not go very far. It was too difficult to travel over or around mountains and bodies of water. This meant that diseases such as plague did not spread easily from one area to another.

▼ *Trading ships carried goods—and diseases—across the oceans to different countries.*

Traveling Diseases

This changed when people developed ways to travel longer distances on water and on land. They began to trade goods with people who lived far away. As people came into contact with each other more often, so did disease.

"The plague started from the Egyptians ... then it divided and moved in one direction ... and spread over the whole world, always moving forward."

Procopius, a writer in the sixth century

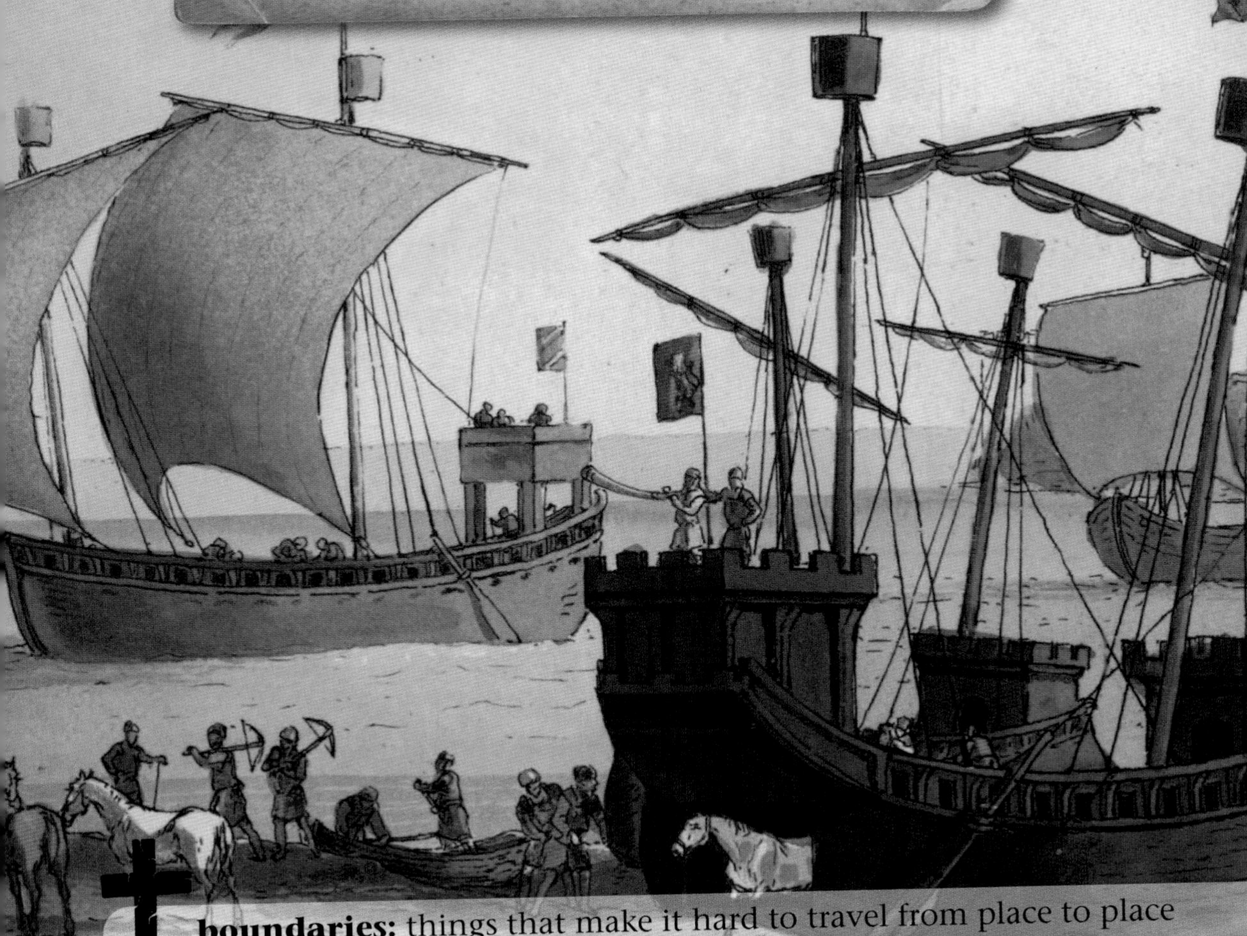

boundaries: things that make it hard to travel from place to place

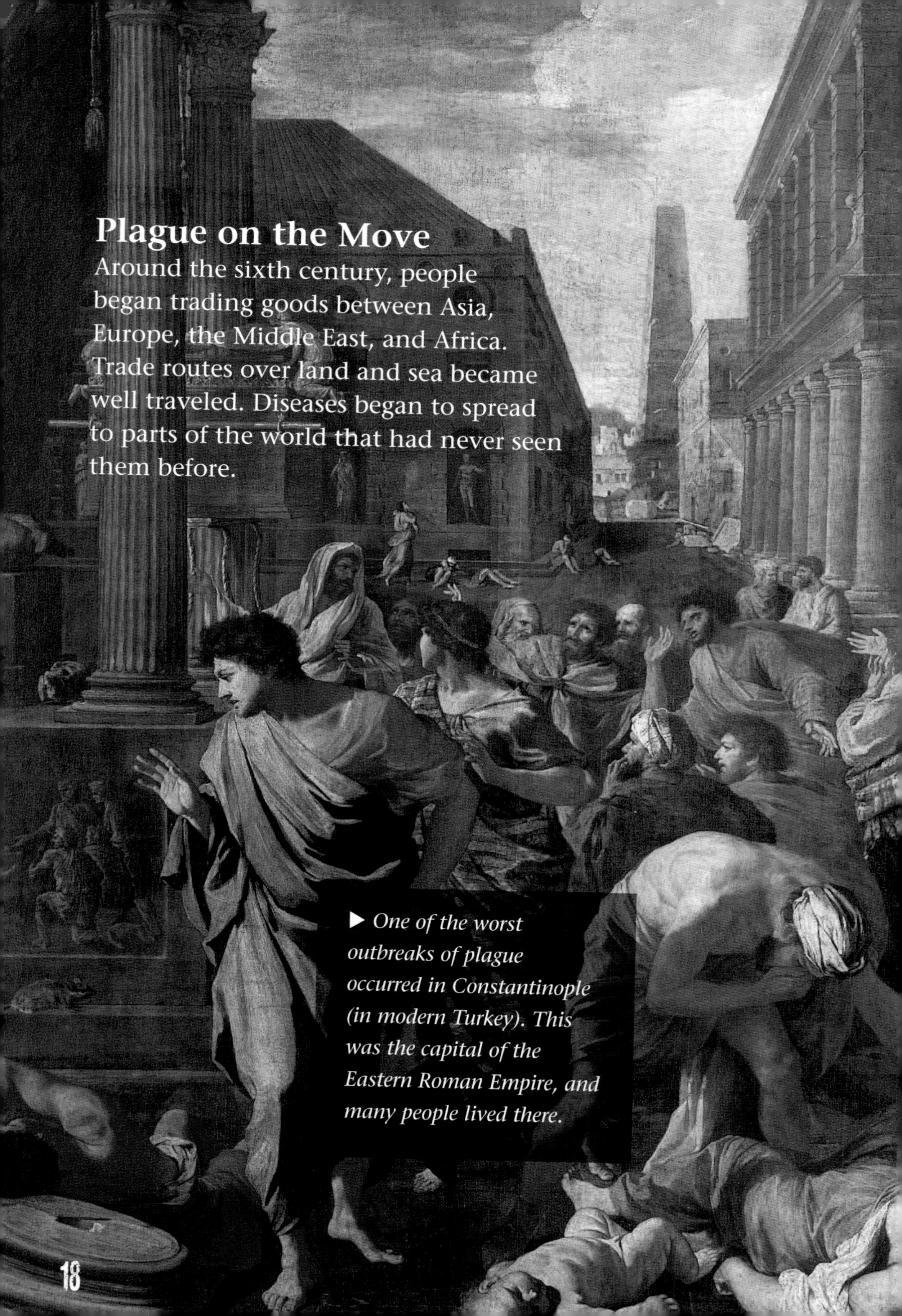

Plague on the Move

Around the sixth century, people began trading goods between Asia, Europe, the Middle East, and Africa. Trade routes over land and sea became well traveled. Diseases began to spread to parts of the world that had never seen them before.

▶ *One of the worst outbreaks of plague occurred in Constantinople (in modern Turkey). This was the capital of the Eastern Roman Empire, and many people lived there.*

The First Outbreak

In 540 C.E., plague-carrying rats arrived in Europe on ships from Africa. The rats climbed to shore from the ropes that tied ships to the docks. More than 25 million people around the world died in the first worldwide **pandemic** of plague. Named after the Roman emperor, it became known as the Plague of Justinian.

> **"The whole human race came near to being entirely destroyed ... the tale of dead reached five thousand each day, and again it even came to ten thousand and still more than that."**
>
> Procopius

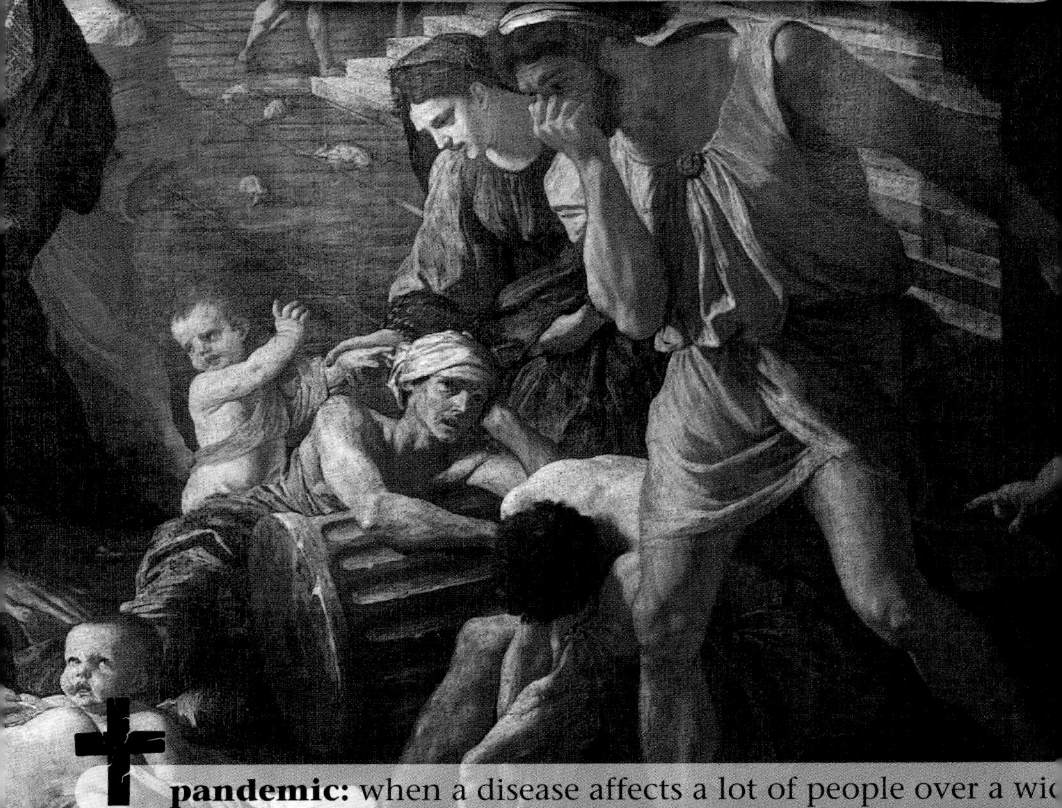

pandemic: when a disease affects a lot of people over a wi

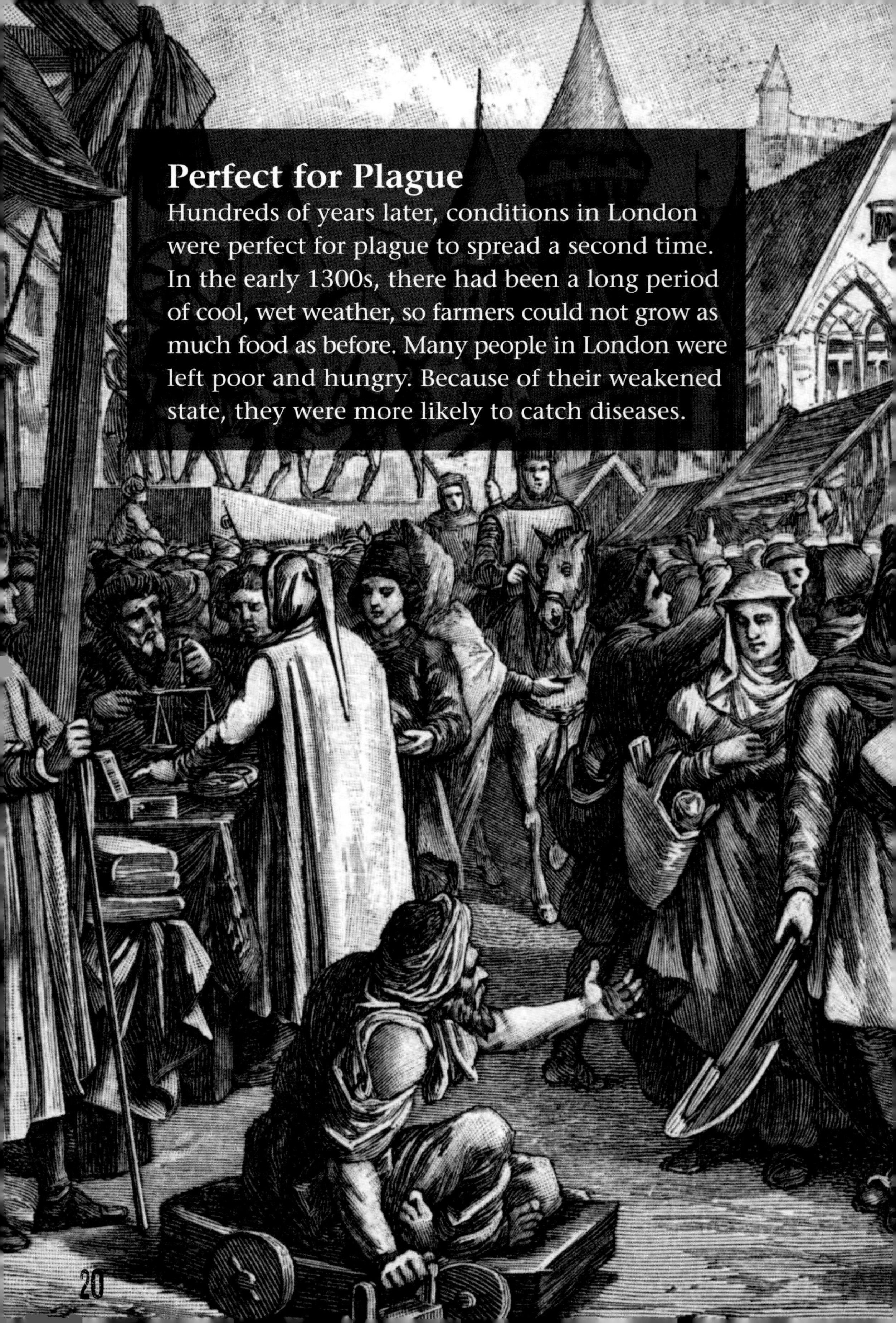

Perfect for Plague

Hundreds of years later, conditions in London were perfect for plague to spread a second time. In the early 1300s, there had been a long period of cool, wet weather, so farmers could not grow as much food as before. Many people in London were left poor and hungry. Because of their weakened state, they were more likely to catch diseases.

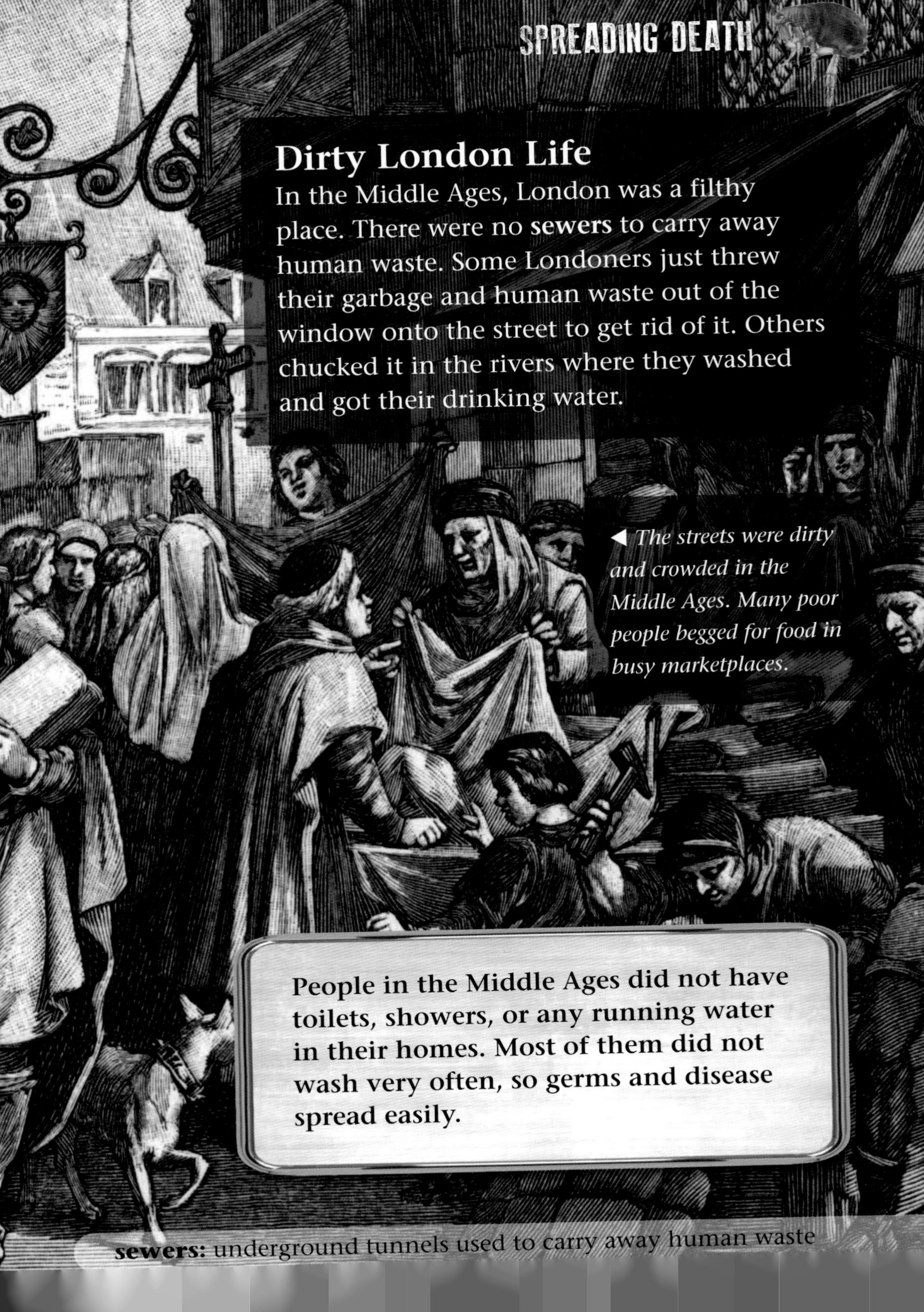

Dirty London Life

In the Middle Ages, London was a filthy place. There were no **sewers** to carry away human waste. Some Londoners just threw their garbage and human waste out of the window onto the street to get rid of it. Others chucked it in the rivers where they washed and got their drinking water.

◄ *The streets were dirty and crowded in the Middle Ages. Many poor people begged for food in busy marketplaces.*

People in the Middle Ages did not have toilets, showers, or any running water in their homes. Most of them did not wash very often, so germs and disease spread easily.

sewers: underground tunnels used to carry away human waste

The Second Wave

Caravans of Death

Caravans were large groups of **merchants** who traveled together. They journeyed from Asia in the east to Europe in the west to sell their goods. Caravans brought with them spices, cloth, grain—and the deadly plague. In the 1300s, this caused a new pandemic of the disease.

▶ *Caravans of traders carried goods on camels and horses from countries in the east along a huge network of trade routes called the Silk Road.*

The Second Pandemic

This second wave of plague was even deadlier than the one hundreds of years before. About half the people in Europe died. As plague swept through cities along the Mediterranean Sea, desperate attempts were made to figure out where this disease had come from and how it could be stopped.

"This pestilence [plague] was so powerful that it spread from the ill to the healthy like fire among dry or oily materials."

Giovanni Boccaccio, an Italian writer in the 1300s

merchants: people who sell goods

Plague Beliefs

Many people believed that plague was God's punishment for their sins. Religious hatred often led people to blame others for events that could not be explained such as plague. Some Christians believed that Jews brought the disease west to destroy them. As punishment, thousands of Jewish people were killed.

▲ *This picture shows Jews being burned alive as a punishment for bringing the Black Death to Christians.*

◀ *In 1261, the Catholic Church banned parades by flagellants because their actions were so extreme. They became popular again in the 1300s, however, as people became desperate to find a cure for plague.*

Whip it Away!

In the Middle Ages, religious men called flagellants whipped themselves three times a day so that God would forgive them for their sins. They also **paraded** through the streets and fell to the ground bleeding. Townspeople would wipe the flagellants' holy blood on their faces. They thought this would protect them from plague.

> **"Not just one person in a house died, but the whole household, down to the cats and the livestock, followed their master to death."**
>
> Michele da Piazza, an Italian monk, describing how no life was spared when an infected ship entered his city

paraded: marched in a line

Panic Spreads

People could see that the cities by the sea were the most affected by the Black Death. Many grabbed what they could carry and fled to cities farther inland. But some of them already had plague. When they grew ill, other people caught the disease. In this way, plague kept spreading.

▼ *People who died of the plague were thrown together and carried away in carts to be buried in mass graves called plague pits.*

Stuck in the Cities

Those who could afford to ran away, but many people had no choice but to stay in the infected cities. In London, guards were ordered to board up the homes of the sick. The door would be marked with a cross so people knew that there was death in that house.

"It struck so much fear in the hearts of men and women that ... fathers and mothers **abandoned** their children, as if they were not even theirs."

Giovanni Boccaccio

abandoned: left behind

▲ *This is a picture from a book printed in the Middle Ages. It shows a doctor "bleeding" a patient.*

Strange Cures

Doctors thought that draining a sick person's blood would let out the disease. This was known as bleeding or bloodletting. They put **leeches** on the patient's body or made small cuts in the skin. This treatment only made things worse. People grew weak from blood loss. They were not strong enough to fight off the Black Death.

The Sweet Smell of Death

Cities were filled with the stench of rotting bodies. Some people believed that plague was spread by the awful smells. They thought that if they smelled pretty things, such as flowers or herbs, they might not catch plague. A lot of people carried posies, or small bunches of flowers, with them.

▶ *Doctors wore masks with beaks filled with herbs and spices to prevent them from smelling death.*

Some people thought that eating pieces of the nasty boils called buboes would protect them from plague. Others would drink the pus from buboes to stop them from getting the disease.

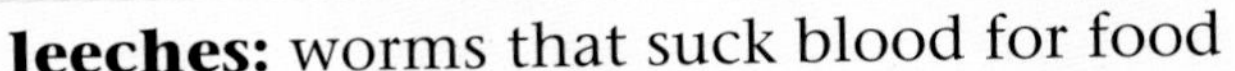

leeches: worms that suck blood for food

A Changed World

The Effects of Plague

Nearly everyone in Europe during that period suffered the effects of plague in one way or another. People either got sick themselves or lost those they loved. So much death changed the way people thought and acted. People began to live each day as if it was their last.

▶ *Some tried to avoid illness by shutting themselves up in their homes. Others lived wildly.*

From Good to Bad

After people died or fled the cities to escape the plague, many homes were left abandoned. Some people moved into the empty houses and lived there. Others stole belongings that had been left behind. They thought the owners were probably dead.

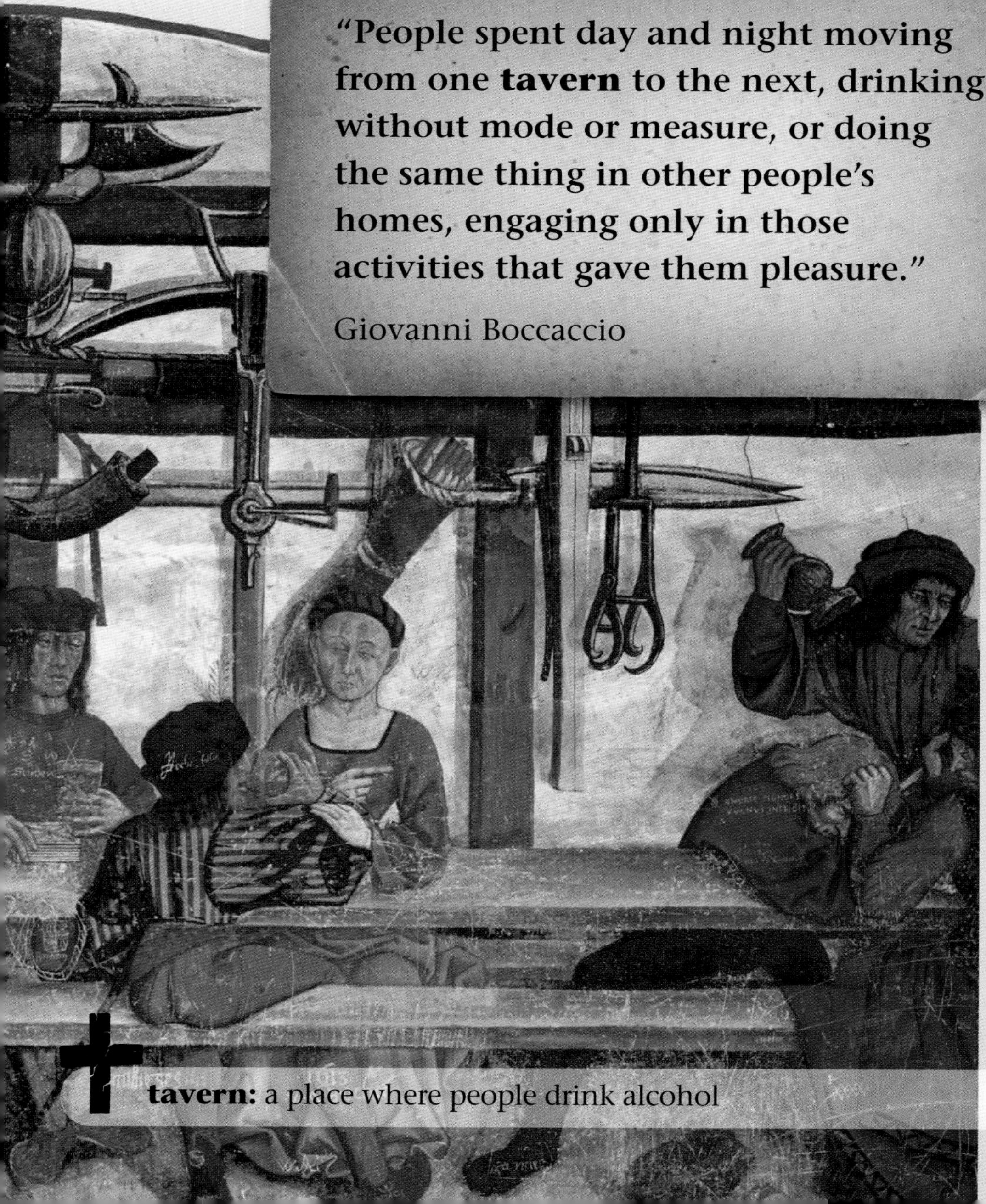

"People spent day and night moving from one tavern to the next, drinking without mode or measure, or doing the same thing in other people's homes, engaging only in those activities that gave them pleasure."

Giovanni Boccaccio

tavern: a place where people drink alcohol

Religious Changes

Some people thought they were being punished by God for being sinners. Yet, children and religious leaders died of the disease, too. Why, they wondered, would God punish the innocent as well as the sinners? People prayed to God to save their sick loved ones—but they died anyway. The plague had shaken many people's faith.

▲ *Many plague paintings show that people felt God had abandoned them. Death appears in this picture as a skeleton in the middle of destruction.*

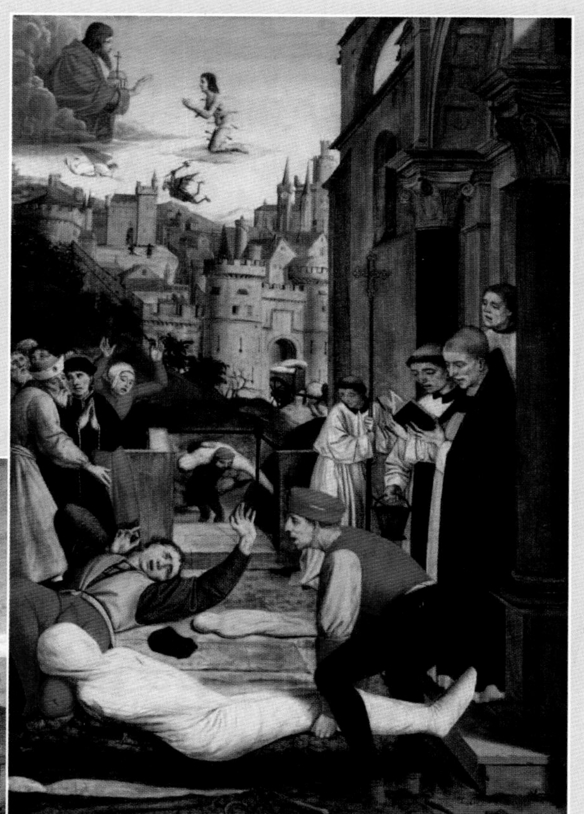

Ungodly Behavior

During the Black Death, a lot of priests left the cities, afraid of catching the disease. People thought that priests should stay and help the sick. Many lost **respect** for them. Most of the priests who did stay caught plague and died. People saw that living a good life would not save them from death.

▲ *Many people prayed to Saint Sebastian for protection from the plague. He is shown here asking God for mercy for people suffering from plague.*

Many priests died or fled during the plague. After the plague went away, the Church offered a lot of money to attract men to the priesthood. But these new priests were not well trained, and many were not very good at the job.

respect: to admire and show special attention to someone

Working Life

Before the plague came, many people were farmers who worked for rich landowners. Most farmers were poor, and a lot of them died during the Black Death. After the plague, there were fewer farmers, so landowners had to pay more money to compete for workers.

▼ *Before the plague, poor farmers worked for low wages. Afterward, they were in great demand, and their lives began to improve.*

After the Plague

Jobs were **plentiful** because so many skilled workers had died. The plague killed all kinds of workers, including priests, butchers, and shopkeepers. After the plague, workers could choose from a number of jobs and get paid more money.

After the plague, peasants could earn up to five times as much money for the same work as they had before the Black Death.

plentiful: when there is a lot of something

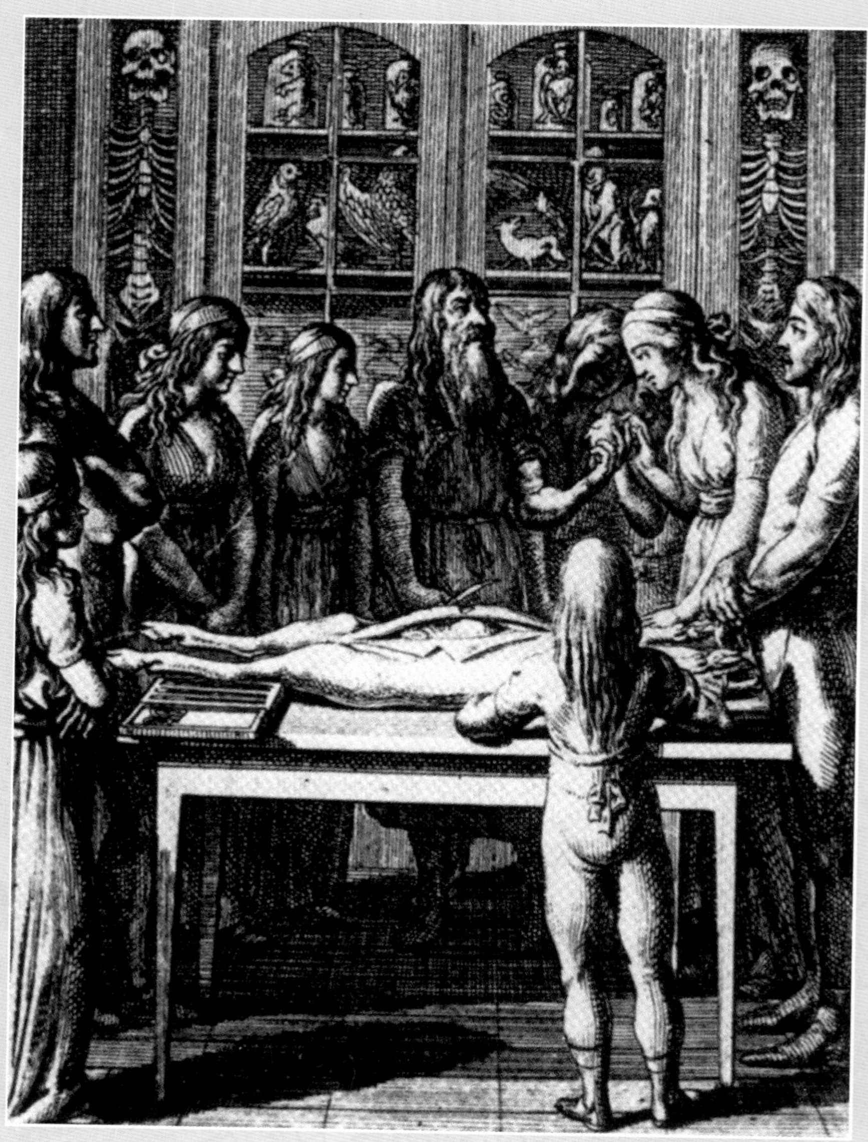

▲ *In the early Middle Ages, doctors cut open pigs' bodies to try and learn about the human body.*

Changes in Medicine

Today, doctors learn about the human body by studying dead bodies. In the 1300s, cutting open human bodies was not allowed. Instead, doctors had to **dissect** pigs' bodies. By the 1500s, the law had changed. Doctors could dissect dead people. They learned much more about disease that way.

Hospital Treatment

There were some hospitals in the Middle Ages. But during the plague, people did not go to hospitals for treatment. Instead, patients were packed into the hospitals just to try to stop others outside from getting sick. After the plague, hospitals became places where doctors treated patients to try to cure them.

▲ *Sometimes the sick were taken to hospitals called pest houses. Most people died there.*

Plague also changed education. Many new schools opened. A lot of these were special schools to train doctors. Being a doctor became a respected profession.

dissect: to cut open a body to find out how it works

Plague Returns

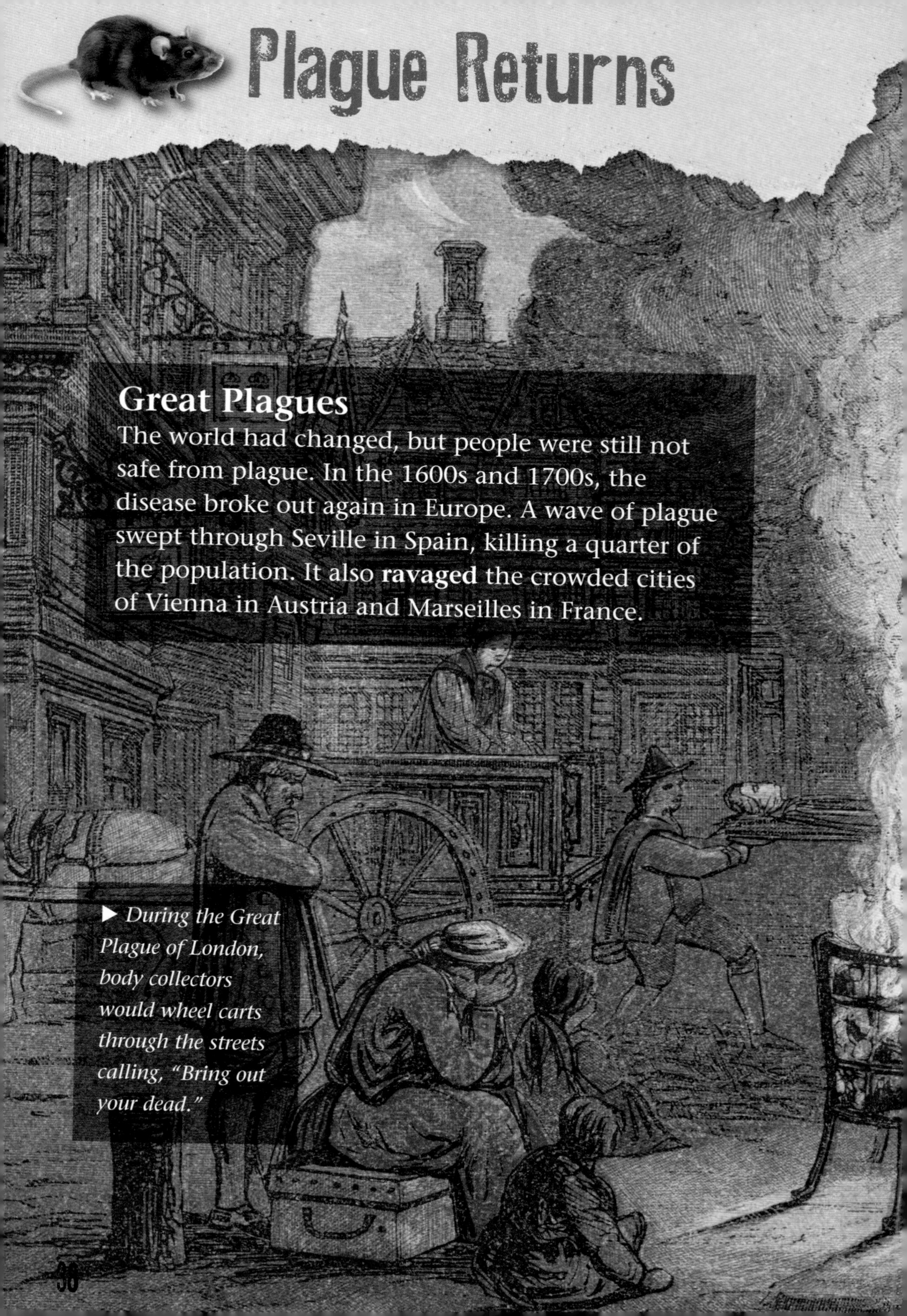

Great Plagues

The world had changed, but people were still not safe from plague. In the 1600s and 1700s, the disease broke out again in Europe. A wave of plague swept through Seville in Spain, killing a quarter of the population. It also **ravaged** the crowded cities of Vienna in Austria and Marseilles in France.

▶ *During the Great Plague of London, body collectors would wheel carts through the streets calling, "Bring out your dead."*

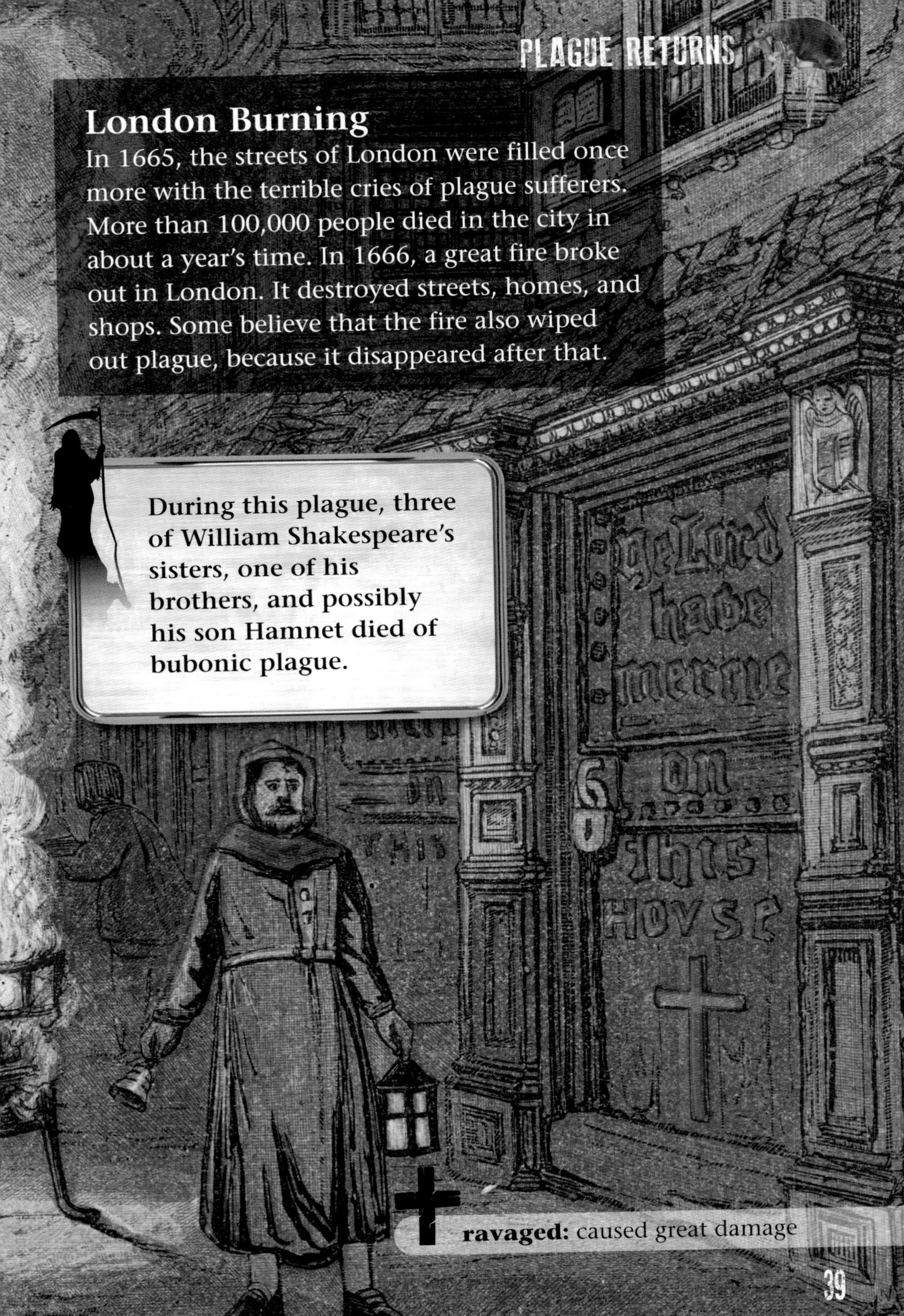

London Burning

In 1665, the streets of London were filled once more with the terrible cries of plague sufferers. More than 100,000 people died in the city in about a year's time. In 1666, a great fire broke out in London. It destroyed streets, homes, and shops. Some believe that the fire also wiped out plague, because it disappeared after that.

During this plague, three of William Shakespeare's sisters, one of his brothers, and possibly his son Hamnet died of bubonic plague.

ravaged: caused great damage

◀ *With the return of plague, artists such as Swiss painter Arnold Bocklin tried to capture people's fear in their art.*

The Next Pandemic

Another plague pandemic broke out in the 1800s. This time it began in China. More than 70,000 people died. Two of the best scientists in the world at the time went to Hong Kong to study the disease. They made many important discoveries, including which **bacteria** caused plague. These scientists also determined that it was rats that carried the disease.

Around the World

Unfortunately, by the time they had made their discoveries, plague had already spread quickly to other countries in the same way it had hundreds of years before. Trade ships brought it to Mumbai in India next. By the 1900s, plague had spread to Australia, the United States, and countries throughout Europe and the Middle East.

▲ *In 1928, the Scottish scientist Alexander Fleming discovered the antibiotic penicillin. Antibiotics kill disease germs and are the only cure for plague.*

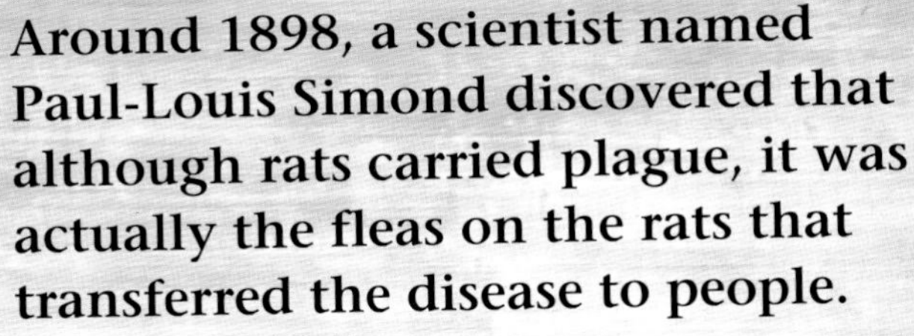

Around 1898, a scientist named Paul-Louis Simond discovered that although rats carried plague, it was actually the fleas on the rats that transferred the disease to people.

bacteria: tiny living things made of a single cell

Plague as a Weapon

Between 1932 and 1945, Japan **experimented** with ways to use plague as a weapon to kill people. Glass containers filled with infected fleas were dropped on cities in China creating epidemics. Thousands of people were killed. Other countries have worked with plague as a weapon, too.

▼ *During World War II, the Japanese army carried out experiments on prisoners of war in this building in China. Scientists tested chemical and biological weapons such as plague.*

Modern Plague Outbreak

In 1994, there was an outbreak of pneumonic plague in Surat, India. Hundreds of people became sick and about 54 died. This kind of plague is a fast killer. People who caught the disease had to find treatment within six hours, or they didn't stand a chance.

▲ *These people are lining up to receive treatment for plague in India in 1994.*

"Less than 48 hours after the first confirmed death, officials ... said that 24 people had died and 137 others were being treated in hospitals."

The New York Times, September 24, 1994

experimented: tested something to see what would happen

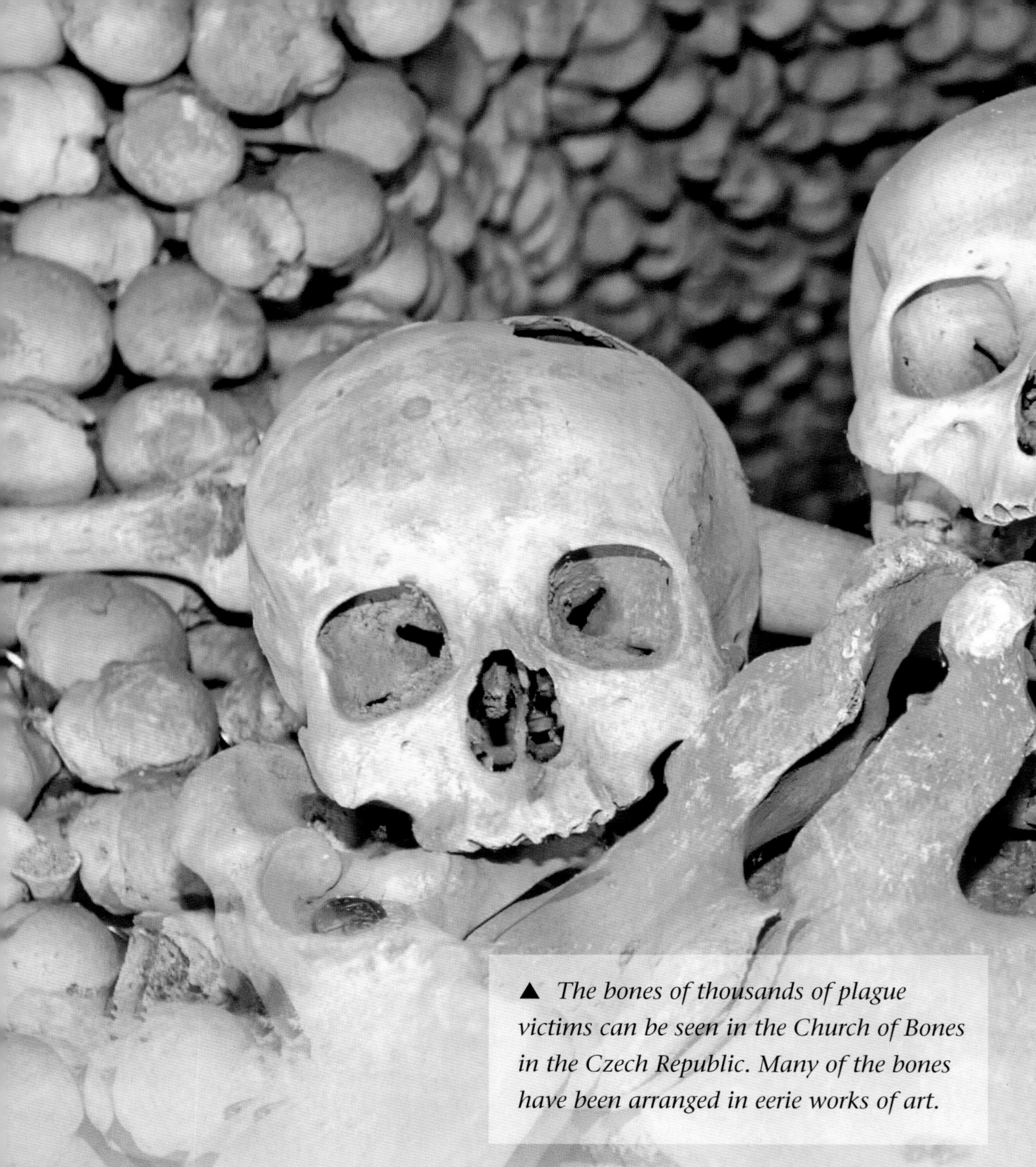

▲ *The bones of thousands of plague victims can be seen in the Church of Bones in the Czech Republic. Many of the bones have been arranged in eerie works of art.*

Plague Today

In August 2012, a seven-year-old girl from Denver, Colorado, caught bubonic plague. She had found and buried a dead squirrel. Doctors thought a flea on the squirrel probably infected her. Her parents rushed her to the hospital. She was given antibiotics and survived.

Still a Threat

Plague might seem like a disease of the past, but it still exists—and it can still kill. People have caught plague in about 30 different countries around the world, including Canada and the United States. Today, if **detected** early enough, it can be treated with antibiotics. People have a much better chance of surviving.

"I thought she had quit breathing ... I thought she had died. I was just running for the ER."

The father of the Colorado girl who caught bubonic plague

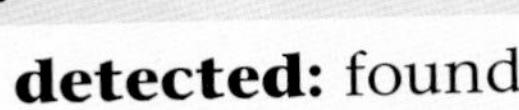

detected: found

Learning More

Books

The Black Death 1347–1350
by Cath Senker
(Heinemann-Raintree, 2007)

The Black Death and Other Putrid Plagues of London
by Natasha Narayan
(Walting Street, 2002)

Bubonic Plague
by Jim Whiting
(Mitchell Lane Publishers, 2006)

Bubonic Plague: The Black Death!
by Stephen Person
(Bearport Publishing, 2010)

Websites

www.eyewitnesstohistory.com/plague.htm
Eyewitness to History: The Black Death, 1348

www.awesomestories.com/disasters/black-death/
Awesome Stories: The Black Death

www.themiddleages.net/plague.html
Bubonic plague in the Middle Ages

Glossary

abandoned Left behind

bacteria Tiny living things made of a single cell

boundaries Things that make it hard to travel from place to place

contagious A disease that is spread by being near an infected person

corpses Dead bodies

detected Found

dissect To cut open a body to find out how it works

experimented Tested something to see what would happen

groin The part of the body between the stomach and thigh

ıfected Having a disease

eches Worms that suck ɔod for food

merchants People who sell goods

pandemic When a disease affects a lot of people over a wide area

paraded Marched in a line

plentiful When there is a lot of something

ravaged Caused great damage

respect To admire and show special attention to someone

rodents Animals with fanglike teeth that are used for chewing

sewers Underground tunnels used to carry away human waste

symptoms The signs that someone has a particular illness

tavern A place where people drink alcohol

Index

Entries in **bold** refer to pictures